Creating Meaningful Tributes

Your Complete Resource for Crafting Personalized Funeral Programs

Christi Anderson

For permissions, inquiries, or additional resources, please visit:

www.funeralprogramsite.com

Published by:

The Funeral Program Site

McKinney, Texas, USA

ISBN: 979-8-9988825-2-4

Cover Design & Interior Layout: The Funeral Program Site

This book is dedicated to every family who has faced the profound journey of saying goodbye. To the mothers, fathers, sisters, brothers, children, spouses, friends, and loved ones—may your memories be preserved with beauty, grace, and the dignity they deserve.

And to those creating funeral programs not just as a task, but as a tribute—your love lives on in every word, every image, every page. May this guide bring clarity in difficult moments, and may it help you honor a life with meaning, care, and heart.

Introduction

Losing someone we love is one of the most difficult experiences we face. Whether expected or sudden, the weight of grief can be overwhelming—and yet, even in sorrow, there's a quiet, sacred responsibility to honor the life that was lived. As families gather to remember, mourn, and celebrate, one of the most meaningful and tangible elements of that farewell is the funeral program.

A funeral program may seem like a small detail in the larger process of planning a service, but its impact is deeply personal. It serves as a guide for the ceremony, a reflection of the loved one's life, and a keepsake that often becomes one of the most cherished mementos people take home. Through its pages, we tell a story. A name, a face, a favorite verse, a memory—it all lives on in this printed tribute.

I founded The Funeral Program Site with the desire to help families during these tender times. Through the years, I've worked alongside people from all walks of life—some grieving quietly, others in a rush to organize a service, and many simply unsure where to begin. What I've learned is that there is no one right way to grieve, and there is no one way to create a funeral program. But what matters most is that it comes from the heart.

This book is for you—whether you're planning a service now, supporting a friend, or preparing in advance for the future. My goal is to offer clarity, creativity, and comfort throughout the process. You'll find guidance on choosing layouts, writing content, understanding printing options, and deciding between professional and DIY approaches. You'll also discover thoughtful ways to personalize a tribute using accessories like bookmarks, prayer cards, and remembrance keepsakes.

Designing a funeral program can be a healing experience. It offers a quiet space to reflect on your loved one's story, gather meaningful memories, and shape them into something beautiful. For some, it's the first time they've paused long enough to cry, smile, or feel the full impact of a life well lived. For others, it's an act of service—a final gift of love.

My hope is that this guide not only answers your practical questions but also encourages you to take comfort in the process itself. May it remind you that grief, while deeply painful, is also a testament to love. And love deserves to be remembered with care.

With heartfelt gratitude,
Christi Anderson
Founder, The Funeral Program Site

Chapter 1

A Brief History of Funeral Programs

Funeral programs, as we know them today, may seem like a modern development, but the tradition of printed materials used to honor the deceased has roots that extend centuries back. Across cultures and eras, people have always sought ways to preserve memory, document ceremony, and share in communal grief. The evolution of the funeral program reflects both advances in technology and the enduring human need to commemorate life.

∽

Origins in Printed Mourning

The earliest forms of printed memorial materials date back to the 17th and 18th centuries in Europe. At that time, funeral announcements and invitations were sent out in the form of engraved cards or letters, often delivered by hand. These formal invitations set the tone for the event and reflected the status of the family. In more affluent circles, printed mourning cards were distributed at or after the service, bearing the name of the deceased, a Bible verse or poem, and sometimes a black border—a visual symbol of mourning.

As printing technology became more accessible in the 19th century, particularly with the invention of the printing press and later the typewriter, memorial cards became more common among middle-class families. These early printed keepsakes were modest in size and content, but they served the same purpose they do today: to offer a tangible remembrance of the departed.

Funeral Programs in the 20th Century

By the early to mid-20th century, funeral programs as we now recognize them began to take shape in the United States. Religious institutions, particularly churches, started producing printed bulletins for funeral services. These included the order of service, names of speakers or clergy, hymns, and scriptures. Initially simple and monochromatic, the programs served more as functional guides than personal tributes.

However, as photocopying and desktop publishing tools became more available in the 1980s and 1990s, funeral programs began evolving into more personalized expressions of remembrance. Families could now include photos, full obituaries, and heartfelt messages in their programs without relying on commercial printers. This marked a significant shift: funeral programs were no longer just informational—they became emotional, artistic, and deeply individualized.

The Digital Age and the Rise of Customization

The 21st century has brought rapid innovation to the funeral program industry. With the rise of personal computers, design software, and digital printing, families now have more control than ever over the look, feel, and content of their memorial pieces. Online templates, downloadable designs, and full-service providers like *The Funeral Program Site* make it possible for anyone, regardless of design experience, to create beautiful tributes from the comfort of home.

Programs have expanded from traditional bifold bulletins to include a variety of formats: gatefolds, booklets, trifolds, memorial cards, and even hybrid designs that reflect individual style. Moreover, accessories like prayer cards, bookmarks, and digital tributes have emerged as complementary pieces that reinforce a unified memorial experience.

Digital versions of funeral programs are also now widely used for virtual services, email distribution, and online memorial pages. These allow for global participation and ensure that the memory of a loved one can reach beyond the physical space of the ceremony.

Cultural and Generational Influence

Throughout history, the design and purpose of funeral programs have been shaped by cultural traditions and generational values. For example, African American funeral traditions have long embraced rich storytelling and visually expressive programs that often include photo collages, spiritual poems, and multi-page booklets. In contrast, minimalist designs remain popular in other cultural contexts where simplicity and symbolism are emphasized over narrative detail.

As new generations take on the task of memorial planning, preferences continue to evolve. Some seek traditional elegance, while others lean toward bold colors, artistic backgrounds, or thematic tributes tied to careers, hobbies, or beliefs. Regardless of format, the intent remains constant: to honor a life and offer solace to those left behind.

Honoring the Past, Embracing the Future

Understanding the history of funeral programs helps us appreciate their enduring importance. What began as a printed announcement has transformed into a meaningful, customizable tribute that bridges generations. It speaks to our need to remember, to share stories, and to give form to our love and grief.

Today, whether designed with software or handcrafted by a family member, the funeral program continues to serve as a tangible legacy. It is a reflection not only of the person we have lost but of the care, creativity, and love of those who remember them.

Chapter 2

The Importance of Personalization in a Funeral Program

When a loved one passes, families are often left searching for meaningful ways to reflect their life and legacy. Amid the decisions and emotions that come with planning a memorial or funeral service, one of the most powerful opportunities to honor that life comes in the form of a personalized funeral program. These programs are far more than schedules or handouts—they are tributes. They are stories in print. And when designed with care and intention, they become lasting keepsakes that speak to the heart.

A funeral program serves both practical and emotional purposes. On a basic level, it guides attendees through the order of service. It introduces speakers, highlights special readings or musical selections, and helps ensure that everything flows smoothly. Yet beyond these logistics, a well-designed funeral program becomes a space to celebrate identity. It allows the person's personality, passions, beliefs, and relationships to shine through the pages—offering a fuller picture than words alone can express during a ceremony.

Personalization can take many forms. Some families choose to include a series of photos that span different life stages, from childhood to adulthood. Others feature handwritten poems, meaningful scripture, or quotes that the loved one cherished. Biographies and tribute paragraphs can bring depth to the program by sharing milestones, career highlights, favorite hobbies, and anecdotes that reflect the character of the individual being remembered. Design choices—such as color palettes, typography, symbols, and themes—can also reflect spiritual beliefs, cultural traditions, or personal style.

One of the most comforting aspects of a personalized funeral program is the way it helps others feel connected. It serves as a shared memory, something tangible that brings people together in their grief while celebrating a common bond with the person they've lost. Guests often leave the service holding onto the program, not just as a guide but as a treasured memento. In the days, months, and even years that follow, these programs can be revisited as a way to reflect, remember, and find peace.

Incorporating personalization into a funeral program can also offer therapeutic value for the family members creating it. Selecting photos, writing out a timeline, and choosing details can become an important part of the grieving process. It's a chance to pause, reflect, and be present with the memories. Creating the program becomes an act of love in itself—a way to ensure that every aspect of the service reflects the essence of the one being honored.

While every life is unique, so too should be the way that life is remembered. A personalized funeral program is a powerful tool that bridges remembrance and design, emotion and function. It becomes a visual and written reflection of a life that mattered, and a symbol of the love that continues even in absence.

Chapter 3

Types of Funeral Programs

When planning a memorial service, one of the most important elements is the printed funeral program. It serves as both a guide and a keepsake, and its format can influence how the life being honored is remembered. Choosing the right type of funeral program depends on several factors—how much information you wish to include, your design preferences, and the tone of the service itself. Fortunately, there are multiple styles and sizes available to suit a wide range of needs.

The most familiar and widely used format is the bifold funeral program. This layout consists of a single sheet of paper folded in half, resulting in four panels: a front cover, two interior pages, and a back cover. Despite its simplicity, the bifold format can hold essential details such as the order of service, obituary, scriptures, and brief acknowledgments. A photo on the front cover is not required, though many families choose to feature one as a personal touch. Others may prefer a more understated approach, opting for elegant artwork, a meaningful quote, or a simple design that reflects the spirit of their loved one. Whether paired with a short biography or tribute placed inside, the clean and structured layout offers a timeless format—perfect for those seeking a graceful balance between simplicity and sentiment.

Another popular option is the trifold funeral program, created by folding one sheet into three equal sections. This results in six distinct panels for content. The extra space accommodates longer readings, multiple poems or scripture verses, detailed biographies, and additional photographs. The trifold format is especially helpful when there are several speakers, musical interludes, or tributes to include. It allows for creative design options while still maintaining a compact size, making it ideal for both hand distribution and mail delivery.

For those seeking a more elegant and dramatic presentation, the gatefold funeral program opens from the center like a pair of doors, revealing a larger central panel inside. This layout is excellent for visual storytelling and photo collages. Its design invites readers to experience the tribute in a more intimate, hands-on way.

One of the most visually dynamic options is the graduated fold funeral program, also known as a step-fold, tiered or tabbed program. These designs feature staggered sections, often labeled for easy navigation. Each tab can represent a specific part of the tribute, such as the obituary, order of service, or family acknowledgments. The format is ideal for longer services and visually organized presentations.

A truly unique option is the combination gatefold-graduated program, which merges the elegance of a gatefold layout with the organizational clarity of a tabbed, graduated fold. This hybrid format opens from the center like a gatefold but reveals layered, stepped pages inside, offering ample space for detailed content and structured navigation. This format is ideal for creative tributes that require both visual impact and clear organization.

For families who want an expansive layout in a more compact form, the long fold funeral program is another compelling option. This format involves folding the sheet vertically (top to bottom) rather than side-to-side. When unfolded, it reveals long, uninterrupted panels ideal for photo collages, poem series, or even a visual timeline. Long folds are especially well-suited for services that include visual storytelling or extended biographical content.

Another innovative layout is the envelope fold funeral program, which folds inward from multiple sides—often resembling the way a letter is sealed in an envelope. This style adds a tactile, surprising element to the presentation. It can be used to conceal a central message, photo collage, or handwritten note, creating a sense of reveal and intimacy. While more complex to produce, envelope folds are visually memorable and perfect for families seeking a truly distinctive tribute.

For memorial services that require comprehensive storytelling, the funeral booklet provides the most space and structure. Typically printed on multiple sheets, folded and stapled along the center, booklets can include biographies, tributes, scriptures, readings, family trees, and numerous photos. Booklets offer flexibility in design and content, allowing additional pages to be included as needed to accommodate extended tributes, multiple photos, or detailed service information. They are ideal for traditional or faith-based services with significant content.

Families seeking a smaller option may prefer a memorial card —a postcard-sized tribute that includes minimal text and one or two photographs. These are perfect for simpler services or when only basic information and a comforting quote or verse need to be shared. Compact and easy to distribute or mail, memorial cards make a wonderful keepsake when a full program isn't necessary.

Each format has its advantages, and the right choice depends on the tone of the service, the quantity of content, and the overall vision the family has for the tribute. Whether simple or elaborate, traditional or modern, a well-chosen layout helps convey love, memory, and legacy in a meaningful way.

As you consider the best format, think not only about what the program will include but how you want it to feel in the hands of those who receive it. The layout should reflect the essence of the person being honored, offering guests not just a printed schedule, but a lasting impression of a life well lived.

Chapter 4

A Visual Guide to Layouts and Styles

W hen planning a memorial service, families are often met with a variety of decisions, both emotional and practical. One of the most meaningful yet frequently overlooked aspects of that planning is the layout of the funeral program. More than just a printed handout, the program plays a vital role in how a loved one's life is remembered, how the service is structured, and how memories are preserved for those in attendance.

The design and format of a funeral program help set the tone for the entire ceremony. It introduces the life story of the person being honored and serves as a tactile reflection of their personality, beliefs, and legacy. Just as every life is different, so too should be the way we present and remember it. Some programs are simple and understated, while others are elaborate, visual, and filled with deeply personal content. The key is selecting the format that best supports the story you want to tell—and the memories you want to share.

Each funeral program layout provides a unique framework for content. Some styles, like the traditional bifold or trifold, are familiar, easy to assemble, and perfect for shorter services. Others, such as the graduated fold, long fold, or hybrid gatefold designs, allow for enhanced storytelling and visual engagement. These more creative options offer space for poems, full-length tributes, photo spreads, and even timelines. Some are designed with practicality in mind; others emphasize artistic expression. And still others serve as compact keepsakes, like memorial cards, that offer a simple but lasting token of remembrance.

As technology and printing capabilities have evolved, so have the possibilities for creating customized funeral programs. What was once a basic, photocopied bulletin has become an opportunity for personalized, full-color tributes—some folded like storybooks, others crafted to unfold in symbolic ways. Families now have the freedom to choose not only what information to include but how they want it presented—visually, structurally, and emotionally.

This visual guide explores the most commonly used and creatively expanded types of funeral programs available today. Each layout described in the following pages includes a visual recommendation for photo placement, helping you see how content might be organized in a real-world design. From the elegance of a gatefold reveal to the practicality of a bifold or the compact simplicity of a memorial card, this chapter aims to help you envision your options before making a decision.

As you browse these styles, consider your loved one's personality, the tone of the service, and the type of content you plan to include. Do you want to highlight many photographs? Is there a full obituary, several poems, or special acknowledgments that need space? Do you prefer something sleek and minimal, or something layered and detailed? The answers to these questions will help guide your choice.

The beauty of today's funeral program designs is that they can be tailored to fit both your vision and your needs. Whether you're working with a designer, using a professional template, or crafting the layout yourself, understanding the range of available formats will help ensure that your program is both meaningful and functional.

The following sections walk through each style in detail, with suggested photo placements to inspire your creativity and assist in bringing your tribute to life.

~

Layout and Styles

Bifold Funeral Program
A timeless layout offering elegance, clarity, and tradition.

The bifold funeral program remains one of the most widely used and universally recognized formats for memorial services. Its simple construction—a single sheet of paper folded once down the center—creates four distinct panels: a front cover, two internal pages, and a back panel.

This intuitive layout makes it easy to assemble and even easier for guests to follow, which is why it's often chosen for both religious and non-religious services alike.

The front cover typically features a portrait of the loved one, accompanied by their full name, dates of birth and passing, and a meaningful phrase such as *"In Loving Memory"*, *"A Celebration of Life"*, or a scriptural verse. This introductory panel sets the tone for the service and serves as a visual tribute guests will see and hold throughout the ceremony.

Inside, the left interior panel is most commonly used for the order of service—listing each part of the ceremony from musical selections and readings to the eulogy and closing remarks. The right interior panel often includes a short obituary, biography, or heartfelt message, capturing the essence of the individual's life, relationships, and legacy. Depending on the family's preferences, it may also hold a prayer, poem, or scripture passage. The back panel provides space for additional elements such as acknowledgments, pallbearer names, reception details, or a final quote or expression of gratitude from the family. Some families choose to include a small photo, church logo, or organization emblem here as well.

This four-panel format is printed on standard letter-size paper (8.5" × 11"), making it cost-effective and compatible with home printers or local copy shops. Its versatility allows for black-and-white printing for a more traditional or budget-conscious presentation, or full-color printing for a vibrant, personalized touch.

Minimalist bifold funeral program in a muted green palette with refined border accents and a centered portrait. This elegant design offers a timeless tribute, perfect for intimate services or keepsake displays. Photo credit: The Funeral Program Site.

Bifold funeral program featuring a soft floral background and elegant script title, designed to highlight a cherished photo and key service details. Photo credit: The Funeral Program Site.

Because of its balance of form and function, the bifold funeral program is ideal for families seeking a traditional, dignified, and straightforward layout. It offers enough space for the most essential information while maintaining a clean, organized appearance. Whether handed out at a church, funeral home, or memorial gathering, the bifold program offers a timeless format that preserves memories with grace and simplicity. It is available in three standard sizes—letter, legal, and tabloid—providing flexibility to accommodate different content needs and preferences.

Trifold Funeral Program

A structured and compact, three-panel layout for extended content without added pages.

The trifold funeral program offers a clean, practical, and space-efficient design that provides more room than a standard bifold—without the need for additional pages. Created by folding a single sheet of paper into three equal vertical sections, this layout yields six distinct panels: three on the front side and three on the reverse. This gives families ample space to include a wide range of content in a single, self-contained format.

A variety of tri-fold funeral brochures showcasing elegant and themed designs, including patriotic, religious, and classic floral styles. Each layout provides ample space for a photo, service information, and a meaningful tribute. Photo credit: The Funeral Program Site.

The trifold funeral brochure is well-suited for presenting a traditional order of service in a clear, organized format. Its six-panel design naturally guides the reader through the flow of the service—from the opening welcome or musical prelude, to prayers, scripture readings, eulogies, and musical selections. This layout is ideal for services that follow a structured sequence, offering a thoughtful way to share the program's progression with attendees.

Tri-fold funeral brochure featuring soft floral artwork and multiple photo placements, ideal for sharing a complete life story. A beautifully organized layout that balances personal imagery with written tributes. Photo credit: The Funeral Program Site.

The ample space allows families to maintain both clarity and elegance while honoring the rituals and traditions of a formal memorial. The segmented structure naturally guides the reader from one panel to the next, allowing you to present the story of your loved one's life in a logical and organized flow.

Families often dedicate one panel to the order of service, another to an obituary or biography, and the remaining spaces to poems, thank-you messages, quotes, or photo collages.

Trifold programs are commonly printed in legal size (8.5" × 14") or tabloid size (11" × 17"), which offer more surface area than standard letter-size paper. Legal size is ideal for traditional services with moderate content, while tabloid size allows for larger photos, longer texts, or visually rich backgrounds and design elements.

Unlike booklet formats, trifold programs cannot be expanded by adding pages. Because they are created from a single sheet, what you see is what you get—making planning and design straightforward. This also keeps printing and folding simple, especially for families who are printing programs at home or working with a local print shop.

Visually, trifold funeral programs can range from formal and minimalistic to artistic and colorful. Their column-like layout is perfect for symmetrical photo arrangements or flowing text. Designers often use the center interior panel as the focal point for the obituary or special photo, flanked by supportive content on the side panels.

For families seeking a contained, elegant, and spacious layout without the complexity of multi-page binding or saddle-stitching, the trifold program is a highly effective and polished solution. It combines versatility and simplicity while offering the space needed to fully honor a life well lived.

Gatefold Funeral Program
A visually engaging layout that opens like a story, honoring a life with grace and symmetry.

The gatefold funeral program is a striking and symbolic layout that creates an unfolding experience for the reader. Designed with two outer panels that open from the center like a pair of doors, this format reveals a large, uninterrupted central panel on the inside. This structure mimics the feeling of opening something sacred or important—like a cherished letter or treasured memory —and is particularly meaningful for a memorial setting.

This style is often chosen when families want to make a powerful emotional impression while still maintaining a simple structure. The outer panels serve as a natural space for elegant quotes, scripture verses, or a single portrait image of the loved one, setting the tone for what's inside. When the program is opened, the reader is welcomed into the heart of the tribute—an expansive interior ideal for the life biography or obituary, order of service details, poems, and photo collages.

Gatefold programs are available in legal size (8.5" × 14") and tabloid size (11" × 17"), both offering more design space than a standard letter-size layout. Legal size is suitable for straightforward services with moderate content, while tabloid allows for generous design freedom and works well for families who wish to include multiple photographs or longer tributes.

Floral gatefold funeral program adorned with vibrant yellow roses and soft golden tones. The front and side panels feature personalized photos and memorial details, creating a warm and heartfelt presentation. Photo credit: The Funeral Program Site.

Peaceful gatefold funeral program featuring a vibrant meadow with butterflies and a blue sky backdrop. The outer panels gently open to reveal heartfelt details, offering a serene and uplifting tribute to a cherished loved one. Photo credit: The Funeral Program Site.

The interior panel is the centerpiece of the design—often used to tell the story of the loved one's life, highlight a timeline, or showcase a large portrait or photo collage with a personal message. The wide, open canvas makes it easy to arrange both text and images without visual clutter, offering a balanced and refined presentation.

The gatefold format works beautifully for families who want their funeral program to feel ceremonial or gallery-like, where each fold and reveal feels intentional and reverent. This layout is especially ideal for tributes that are rich in imagery, spiritual messages, or symbolic storytelling.

Its structure also lends itself well to creative themes, such as journeys, transitions, or celebrations of legacy, making it an excellent choice for memorials that focus on hope, peace, and reflection.

While more visually complex than a bifold or trifold, gatefold programs are still printed from a single sheet on either legal or tabloid size paper, making them efficient to produce—especially when professionally scored and folded. The clean presentation and emotional storytelling make this format a standout choice for honoring a life that deserves a moment of pause and admiration. Its unfolding structure creates a sense of reverence and surprise, making each reveal feel intentional and heartfelt.

∾

Graduated Fold (Tabbed) Program
Organized navigation with staggered tabs.

Graduated funeral programs—also known as step-fold, tier or tabbed programs—are a visually layered and highly organized memorial format that helps guide attendees through key parts of the service. With staggered, labeled tabs extending from the edge of each page, this layout not only adds visual interest but also makes it easy to locate specific sections such as "Obituary," "Scripture," "Order of Service," "Tributes," and more. These programs are available with either side tabs or bottom tabs, giving families flexibility in presentation.

Side tabs are vertically aligned along the right-hand edge of the program and come in 1-tab or 3-tab formats, depending on the number of sections being included. Bottom tabs are aligned horizontally across the lower edge of the program and are also available in 1-tab or 3-tab formats, offering a unique and easily accessible alternative to side-tab styles.

Graduated fold programs are printed in a variety of sizes to suit your needs, including:

- **Letter (8.5" × 11")** – Ideal for traditional services and standard content.
- **Legal (8.5" × 14")** – Offers extra vertical space for extended text or full-length poems.
- **Tabloid (11" × 17")** – Best suited for photo-rich layouts or longer formats that require both space and structure. This size allows for full-page image spreads, extended biographies, or detailed service outlines without compromising readability or design balance.

8-sided graduated funeral program with a bottom tab layout, featuring soft lilac florals and elegant gold script. Each labeled section provides easy navigation through the service details, obituary, and loving tributes. Photo credit: The Funeral Program Site.

This format is perfect for services that include multiple contributors or detailed elements, as the clearly labeled tabs act as section dividers, helping guests follow along with ease. Each panel or page within the graduated layout can be fully customized to match the tone and theme of the tribute—whether solemn, celebratory, faith-based, or nature-inspired program—an added touch that elevates it from a simple handout to a cherished keepsake.

*Elegant 8-sided graduated funeral program in soft lavender hues, featuring
staggered side tabs labeled for Order of Service, Obituary, and Tribute. A
graceful layout for honoring a cherished life with beauty and organization.
Photo credit: The Funeral Program Site.*

4-sided graduated funeral program with soft green hues and floral accents, ideal for a gentle, heartfelt tribute. Features a side tab with the loved one's name and space for a cherished photo on the front cover. Photo credit: The Funeral Program Site.

Visually, the graduated fold gives a professional, publication-quality appearance that feels both polished and personal. Graduated funeral programs feature staggered customizable tabs that create a layered, easy-to-navigate format, often labeled with sections like "Obituary," "Order of Service," or "Tribute." While visually appealing and well-organized, this layout is not recommended for adding additional pages due to the complexity of its assembly.

The precise alignment required for the tabs means that expanding beyond the standard format can lead to printing or folding inconsistencies, making the assembly process more difficult. For this reason, it's best to plan the content carefully within the available tabbed pages to maintain the professional appearance and structural integrity of the program.

Whether you choose a single tab to highlight a specific feature, or a 3-tab layout to segment the memorial content, the graduated funeral program offers an intuitive and elegant way to guide loved ones through remembrance. Each tab serves as a gentle visual cue, helping guests navigate the story of a life with ease and reflection.

Combination Gatefold-Graduated Program
A premium hybrid layout for dynamic presentation and guided remembrance.

The combination gatefold and graduated program is a truly distinctive and high-impact memorial layout that blends two powerful design formats: the visual drama of a gatefold and the functional organization of a graduated (or tabbed) fold. The result is a premium, multi-panel tribute that offers both emotional depth and clarity in structure—ideal for families who want to create a highly personalized, immersive remembrance experience.

Caption: *Tropical-themed combination gatefold and graduated funeral program featuring serene ocean imagery and labeled tabs for Order of Service, Obituary, and Tribute. A vibrant, storybook-style layout that brings warmth and peacefulness to the memorial. Photo credit: The Funeral Program Site.*

When closed, the gatefold-style outer panels meet in the center like two elegant doors. This creates a sense of ceremony as the reader opens the program, much like revealing a story or unveiling a cherished memory. Inside, you'll find graduated or staggered interior panels, each labeled to your specifications or headed to guide the reader through sections such as "Obituary," "Order of Service," "Poems," "Tributes," or "Photos."

This tiered interior structure allows readers to navigate the content with ease, while the gatefold cover adds visual sophistication and symbolism—representing the passage from one chapter of life to the next. It's a format that works especially well when the tribute is designed around a thematic or narrative flow, making it perfect for creative storytelling, memorials for artists or educators, or celebrations of life that include multiple contributors and content types.

Because of its complexity, this layout is most often professionally printed and assembled, ensuring precise folds, clean tab alignment, and a polished appearance. It is typically printed on larger sheets such as legal or tabloid size to accommodate both the fold mechanics and sufficient space for content. The use of durable paper stock and strategic scoring helps maintain crisp folds and longevity, making it a lasting keepsake for family and guests.

Visually, this format offers abundant room for full-page photo spreads, collage layouts, and detailed text, while keeping everything well-organized. Its refined appearance and thoughtful structure make it an excellent choice for those seeking a standout piece that honors a life with elegance, emotion, and clarity.

∼

Long Fold Funeral Program
A vertical layout designed for uninterrupted storytelling.

The long fold funeral program offers a distinct and elegant alternative to traditional side-fold formats. Folded vertically from top to bottom, this layout opens to reveal an extended canvas— perfect for organizing content in a flowing, narrative style. Its taller proportions allow for uninterrupted visual storytelling, making it especially well-suited for layouts that benefit from vertical sequencing.

This format is ideal for showcasing a life timeline, from birth and childhood to key milestones, family, and legacy. Photos can be arranged chronologically down the page, allowing viewers to visually journey through a person's life as they scroll or unfold. The vertical orientation also lends itself beautifully to poetic layouts, single-column scripture verses, or cascading obituary segments.

Printed on a single sheet of letter size paper, the long fold can accommodate two to four vertical panels depending on your layout and print setup. For example, a letter-size sheet folded lengthwise offers two long panels (front and back), while accordion folds allow for more segmented storytelling across multiple sections.

Visually, long fold programs stand out from the standard booklet-style format, making them an excellent choice for those looking to honor their loved one in a more modern or artistic way. The tall shape pairs well with full-length portrait photos, elegant typography, and subtle background imagery such as floral Long fold funeral programs printed in soft pastel parchment tones, folded top to bottom for a vertical layout. Ideal for displaying a life timeline or cascading photo tribute in a modern, elegant presentation.

Long fold funeral programs with a classic parchment design, folded vertically for a tall, elegant presentation.

Because this format is less common, it can also feel more personal and intentional—as though the tribute itself unfolds slowly, giving space to every word, every image, and every reflection. Whether used for a traditional memorial or a celebration of life, the long fold funeral program offers a clean, thoughtful design that captures the emotional arc of a life remembered. Its elongated layout allows for creative storytelling, flowing naturally from one section to the next. This design invites mourners to linger, reflect, and truly connect with the essence of the person being honored.

~

Envelope Fold Program
Creative and tactile—unfolds like a personal letter.

The envelope fold funeral program is one of the most unique and visually engaging formats available. Unlike traditional folds that open in a linear or book-like fashion, this layout folds inward from multiple directions, often from all four sides—top, bottom, left, and right—much like the flaps of an envelope.

Once opened, it reveals a central panel that typically holds the most meaningful content, such as a full-page photo, a poem, or a heartfelt message.

This unfolding sequence offers a symbolic and intimate experience, as if the recipient is unwrapping something deeply personal. Each layer can hold its own content, allowing for a storytelling progression: perhaps a quote on the outer fold, a photo collage on the inner flaps, and a written tribute or scripture in the center.

Envelope fold programs are especially well-suited for personalized, poetic, or artistic tributes. They are commonly used in memorials that celebrate a creative individual or to highlight a theme such as nature, spirituality, or a life journey. The central reveal often serves as a dramatic moment during a service, inviting emotional connection and reverence.

Landscape-style envelope fold funeral program featuring a serene countryside background and coordinating "Forever In Our Hearts" closure flap. A warm and memorable design that unfolds into a personalized celebration of life. Photo credit: The Funeral Program Site.

This unique layout also lends itself well to personalization through creative embellishments, such as patterned paper, decorative closures, or thematic background designs that complement the life being celebrated. Because of its envelope-style presentation, this program type can double as a keepsake—often treasured long after the service.

When paired with high-quality paper stock and thoughtful design elements, the envelope fold becomes more than just a program; it becomes a tangible expression of remembrance, one that unfolds both literally and emotionally for those who hold it.

Because of the complex folds and layered structure, this

format is best suited for professionally printed and scored paper with careful assembly. The layout can be printed on a single tabloid-size sheet (11" × 17") or designed using creative cuts and folds on letter or legal paper, depending on the intended size. It's ideal for those seeking a non-traditional layout that evokes warmth, symbolism, and surprise.

∾

Funeral Booklet
A multi-page format for in-depth tributes.

Funeral booklets are ideal for services that require space to share a more comprehensive tribute. These multi-page programs are created by folding multiple sheets of paper and binding them with staples (saddle stitching) along the center fold.

This format allows for clear organization of a large amount of content, making it perfect for longer memorial services, cultural ceremonies, or celebrations of life that include many contributors.

Booklets are typically printed in letter (8.5" × 11"), legal (8.5" × 14"), or tabloid (11" × 17") sizes, depending on how much space is needed and how visually impactful the family wants the program to be. The final size, once folded, will be half of the full sheet size —so a tabloid-size sheet folded in half will result in a large 8.5" × 11" booklet.

These programs can include extended biographies, multiple tributes, scriptures, eulogies, song lyrics, acknowledgments, photo pages, and even timelines or family trees. The structured layout provides space for headers, section breaks, and full-page spreads, offering a polished and elegant presentation.

Funeral booklets are an excellent choice for families who wish to include a more extensive tribute, offering ample space for multiple sections such as a full obituary, order of service, poems, scripture readings, and photo collages. Commonly produced using several sheets of paper folded and saddle-stitched along the center, booklets provide a clean and organized format that can be easily expanded based on the family's needs.

In addition to their spacious layout, funeral booklets are available in various sizes—letter, legal, and tabloid—offering flexibility in both design and presentation. Their multi-page structure makes them particularly suitable for formal services, celebrations of life, or culturally rich ceremonies that include detailed elements. Whether simple or elaborate, funeral booklets serve as cherished keepsakes that loved ones can hold onto long after the service concludes.

Floral-themed bifold funeral program featuring a golden background with butterflies and vibrant blossoms. Includes space for a tribute photo and personalized service details, with coordinating interior pages for poems and remembrances. Photo credit: The Funeral Program Site.

Funeral booklets are an excellent choice for families who wish to include a more extensive tribute, offering ample space for multiple sections such as a full obituary, order of service, poems, scripture readings, and photo collages. Commonly produced using several sheets of paper folded and saddle-stitched along the center, booklets provide a clean and organized format that can be easily expanded based on the family's needs.

Funeral booklet with elegant lavender rose accents and bold "In Loving Memory" title, perfect for a soft, floral tribute. Includes space for a cherished photo and essential service details. Photo credit: The Funeral Program Site.

In addition to their spacious layout, funeral booklets are available in various sizes—letter, legal, and tabloid—offering flexibility in both design and presentation. Their multi-page structure makes them particularly suitable for formal services, celebrations of life, or culturally rich ceremonies that include detailed elements. Whether simple or elaborate, funeral booklets serve as cherished keepsakes that loved ones can hold onto long after the service concludes.

Because of their bound format, funeral booklets are often seen as keepsake-quality items—designed not only to guide guests through the ceremony but to be treasured and revisited in the years to come. Whether printed at home or professionally produced, funeral booklets deliver a powerful and lasting tribute that truly tells the story of a life lived.

Memorial Card

A compact tribute for minimal content. Memorial cards are a beautifully simple and practical way to honor a loved one when only a small amount of content is needed.

Typically postcard-sized, these cards feature a single photo of the deceased on the front, along with their name, birth and passing dates, and a short quote, scripture, or poem that reflects their life or values. Despite their compact size, memorial cards hold deep meaning and are often cherished by attendees as keepsakes that can be easily carried, framed, or stored in a memory box.

Folded memorial card featuring a heavenly blue sky design with radiant cross and personalized photo. A thoughtful and spiritual tribute for honoring a loved one's life and faith. Photo credit: The Funeral Program Site.

Memorial cards come in two main styles: flat or folded. Flat memorial cards are printed four per standard letter-size sheet (8.5" × 11"), with content on the front and, optionally, the back.

Caption: *Flat memorial card featuring a peaceful cornfield backdrop and a personalized portrait, ideal for honoring those who cherished nature, farming, or rural life. A unique and heartfelt tribute design. Photo credit: The Funeral Program Site.*

Folded memorial cards are slightly larger when opened and are typically printed two per sheet, allowing space for a small obituary or additional verses inside. The folded option adds a layer of intimacy and dimension, making it ideal for those who want a miniaturized program format without the complexity of a larger layout.

These cards are especially useful at informal gatherings, graveside services, or for mailing to individuals who couldn't attend in person. Their smaller footprint makes them easy to distribute and cost-effective to print in quantity.

Memorial cards offer a compact yet meaningful way to honor

a loved one, making them ideal for handing out at services, mailing to distant friends and family, or including in thank-you notes. They often feature a photo, name, dates, and a short message, prayer, or quote that captures the essence of the individual being remembered.

In addition to their versatility, memorial cards are available in both flat and folded styles and are typically printed two or four per sheet on letter-size paper. Their small size makes them easy to carry or keep in a wallet, Bible, or memory box. Whether used alone or as a complement to a larger funeral program, these cards provide a personal and lasting tribute in a format that's both accessible and beautifully simple.

Chapter 5

Common Elements to Include in a Program

A thoughtfully prepared funeral program can serve as a meaningful bridge between memory and mourning. It not only helps attendees follow the progression of a memorial service but also preserves the legacy of the loved one being honored. While every program is unique, most include a set of core elements that provide structure, emotional resonance, and a lasting keepsake for those in attendance.

The cover is often the most visible and symbolic part of the program. It typically features the full name of the deceased, along with their birth and passing dates. A photograph—usually a formal portrait or a cherished candid—adds a personal touch and invites connection at first glance. Some families also choose to include a meaningful quote, a favorite scripture verse, or a phrase like "Celebrating the Life Of" or "In Loving Memory." The cover design sets the tone for the rest of the content, whether elegant, spiritual, floral, or minimalist.

Inside the program, the order of service plays a central role. This section outlines the sequence of events during the memorial or funeral ceremony. It often includes details such as welcome messages, prayers, readings, musical performances, eulogies, and acknowledgments. Clearly listing each part of the service helps guests know what to expect and follow along respectfully. It also provides structure and flow for the officiant or family members who are leading the program.

Another vital element is the obituary or life summary. This narrative portion provides a written account of the individual's life—highlighting key milestones, family relationships, career achievements, hobbies, and personal values. A well-written obituary tells a story, capturing not just the facts but the spirit of the person. Some programs feature a condensed version, while others expand it across multiple pages or sections. In either case, it serves as a tribute that helps future generations remember and understand their loved one.

Many families choose to include photos throughout the program, either in the form of a collage or as individually placed images between sections. These visuals help evoke memories and emotions, allowing guests to reflect on joyful moments and shared experiences. Depending on space, some programs include childhood pictures, wedding portraits, family gatherings, or professional accomplishments. If the program does not require a large amount of written content, dedicating a full page to a photo collage can be a beautiful and impactful alternative. These visual tributes help fill the space meaningfully while enhancing the emotional tone of the program.

Scripture verses, poems, or song lyrics are also commonly included in funeral programs and tributes. These elements serve not only as comforting words but as emotional touchstones that can bring healing, perspective, and a sense of spiritual connection during a time of grief. A well-chosen passage has the power to speak directly to the heart, reminding attendees of the values, hopes, or faith of the person being remembered. Whether it's a Bible verse that was frequently quoted, a hymn that was especially meaningful, or a favorite poem that reflects the individual's outlook on life, including these personal expressions can add a layer of authenticity and emotional depth to the service.

Bible verses, in particular, often provide reassurance to grieving families. Words of promise, peace, and eternal life can offer hope in the midst of sorrow and serve as a reminder that their loved one is at rest. For those grounded in faith, these verses can help strengthen their trust in God's presence during a difficult season. When shared thoughtfully, they can unite the family in a shared sense of spiritual comfort and provide enduring encouragement well beyond the day of the service.

Acknowledgments and expressions of gratitude often appear near the end of the program. This section gives families an opportunity to thank those who supported them during their time of loss—such as clergy, friends, hospice workers, or pallbearers. It can also include an invitation to a repast or reception following the service, or instructions for those viewing remotely.

Depending on the length and format of the program, families may also include a favorite recipe, a timeline of life events, handwritten notes, or messages from grandchildren. These creative elements make the program even more personal and memorable, offering opportunities for customization when standard content is limited.

Finally, the back cover often features a closing sentiment. This could be a final photo, a prayer or popular in loving memory poem, a quote about life and remembrance, or a simple phrase like "Forever in Our Hearts." The funeral service provider or home entrusted with the arrangements is often noted at the end of the back page of the program. This serves as a respectful acknowledgment of their role in guiding the family through the planning process and offering professional care during a sensitive time. Including the funeral home's name, logo, or contact information is not only customary but can also be helpful for guests who may wish to send follow-up inquiries, express gratitude, or refer others in the future. It also adds a formal touch to the program's overall presentation.

Some families choose to leave this space blank for guests to write their own thoughts or signatures during the service.

While there is no one "correct" way to design a funeral program, these common elements provide a strong foundation for creating a meaningful and respectful tribute. The beauty of a personalized program lies in its ability to be tailored to the individual—blending structure with story, information with emotion. When approached with care, the program becomes more than a guide for the day—it becomes a keepsake of love, memory, and legacy.

~

Chapter 6

How to Choose the Right Design

Selecting the right design for a funeral program is one of the most meaningful steps in honoring a loved one. The layout, style, and imagery you choose set the tone for how the person's life will be remembered during the service and long after. With so many design options available today, this process can feel overwhelming at first. However, with a little guidance and reflection, families can choose a design that feels personal, appropriate, and truly representative of the individual being remembered.

The first factor to consider is the tone of the service itself. Is it a traditional, religious ceremony held in a church? Is it a celebration of life in a casual or outdoor setting? The tone can guide your choice between formal, spiritual designs and more relaxed or colorful styles. For instance, a traditional program might feature soft backgrounds, script fonts, and religious symbols. A celebration-of-life style might lean toward vibrant colors, playful typography, and a design theme that reflects the loved one's personality—such as nature, music, sports, or travel.

Next, consider how much content you plan to include. A short, intimate service may only require a bifold design with four panels, while a larger service involving multiple speakers, extended tributes, and numerous photos might benefit from a trifold, gatefold, or booklet layout. The chosen format should comfortably accommodate the text and images without looking overcrowded or sparse. It's helpful to gather all the content first—such as the obituary, order of service, poems, and photos—before committing to a layout.

Color palette plays an important role in setting the emotional tone. Soft pastels and muted tones often evoke peace and serenity, while deep blues, burgundy, and gold can convey elegance and tradition. Bright colors can be uplifting and reflect a joyful personality, especially in celebration-of-life services. If the deceased had a favorite color, incorporating it subtly into the design adds a personal touch.

The theme of the program can also be guided by the loved one's interests or background. For example, a floral theme might suit someone who loved gardening, while a scenic mountain or ocean background could reflect a deep connection to nature. Military, patriotic, or cultural-themed programs are available for veterans and individuals with strong heritage or national pride. Selecting a design that connects visually to the person's life story helps attendees feel a stronger emotional connection.

Typography choices matter more than most people realize. Serif fonts like Garamond or Times New Roman lend a classic, refined feel, while sans-serif fonts like Helvetica or Arial provide a clean, modern look. Script fonts can add a personal, elegant touch, but should be used sparingly to maintain readability—especially for older attendees. Choose font sizes that are easy to read, and balance headers, body text, and captions so that the program flows naturally from section to section.

Don't forget to factor in how the program will be printed or distributed. If the service is virtual or includes remote attendees, digital designs that look good on screens are important. In that case, horizontal or landscape-style layouts can work especially well. For printed programs, consider how they'll be folded, stapled, or inserted into folders. Paper type and print quality can elevate even the simplest design.

When in doubt, many families benefit from reviewing examples or templates before making a decision. Looking through options that feature different layouts, themes, and visual styles can help clarify what feels "right." Some families find that the chosen design practically selects itself—because it simply looks and feels like their loved one. That kind of emotional resonance is one of the most important signs that the right choice has been made.

In the end, choosing a design is not just a visual decision—it's a storytelling decision. The images, layout, and colors you select combine with words and memories to create a tangible expression of a person's life. A well-designed funeral program is not only a guide for the service; it's a reflection of identity, values, and love. Whether simple or elaborate, modern or traditional, the best design is the one that helps you tell the story you want to preserve.

Chapter 7

Choosing the Right Approach

Done-for-You Services vs. Do-It-Yourself

When planning a funeral program, families often face the decision between utilizing professional, done-for-you services or embarking on a do-it-yourself (DIY) approach. Each option offers distinct advantages and considerations, and the best choice depends on factors such as time constraints, budget, desired level of customization, and personal comfort with design and printing processes.

Done-for-You Services: Convenience and Professionalism

Using a professional service for funeral program creation offers several key advantages that can bring peace of mind during a difficult time. One of the primary benefits is time-saving—these services manage every aspect of the design and printing process, allowing families to focus on arrangements and emotional support. Additionally, expert designers bring a high level of skill and experience, producing polished, visually appealing programs that respectfully honor the life of the deceased.

Professional printing also guarantees quality assurance, resulting in high-end materials and a refined finish that makes each program a lasting keepsake. Many providers further enhance their value by offering comprehensive packages, which often include matching prayer cards, bookmarks, and thank-you notes, ensuring a cohesive and thoughtful memorial presentation.

While professional services offer convenience and high-quality results, there are some considerations to keep in mind. Cost can be a significant factor, as these services are often more expensive than do-it-yourself (DIY) options—posing a challenge for families managing expenses during a difficult time.

Potential shipping or courier delays are an important consideration when selecting done-for-you services, especially for time-sensitive materials like funeral programs. Since memorial services often occur within a short window, any delay in delivery could impact the availability of these essential items.

This makes it crucial to plan ahead and confirm production and shipping timelines with your provider. Choosing expedited delivery options or working with a service that offers reliable turnaround times can help ensure that your printed programs arrive on schedule and are ready for distribution at the service.

Additionally, although professionals aim to reflect the personality and spirit of the deceased, some families may feel a stronger emotional connection by taking part in creating the program themselves.

DIY: Do-It-Yourself Funeral Program Creation

Choosing a DIY approach brings its own set of advantages, particularly in terms of personalization and affordability. Families can fully customize the design with meaningful touches like favorite colors, cherished quotes, and personal photographs, resulting in a tribute that feels truly unique. DIY methods are also budget-friendly, especially when using downloadable templates or preprinted funeral paper and home printing, which helps minimize costs. Moreover, this approach offers flexibility and control, allowing families to adjust content and layout on their own timeline without being bound to external deadlines.

Types of DIY funeral programs include downloadable online templates and preprinted funeral paper. Downloadable templates are pre-designed digital files that can be personalized with photos, text, and service details, then printed at home or a local print shop. These offer flexibility and creative control, making them a popular choice for families who want a custom look while managing costs.

Preprinted funeral paper, on the other hand, comes with a decorative front cover already printed, often featuring a scenic or themed design. This option requires no personalization on the front and works well for those looking to print only the inside and back panels—ideal for black and white printing. It provides a simple and elegant solution for creating programs with minimal design effort.

Despite its benefits, the DIY approach also comes with potential drawbacks that families should consider. Creating a funeral program from scratch can be time-consuming, adding pressure during an already emotionally and logistically challenging period. The process demands careful attention to layout, content, and printing, which may not be feasible for those juggling multiple responsibilities.

Additionally, technical skills are often required to achieve a polished result. Proficiency with design software and familiarity with printing tools are essential for producing a program that meets expectations. Even with the right tools, quality can vary significantly—home printers may fall short of delivering the crisp images and vibrant colors offered by professional printing services, and the choice of paper can further influence the program's overall durability and visual appeal.

Deciding between done-for-you services and a DIY approach ultimately comes down to your family's unique needs, preferences, and circumstances. Time availability is a key factor— if the service is approaching quickly and there's little time to prepare, professional services can significantly reduce stress and ensure everything is completed promptly. On the other hand, budget constraints and potential shipping delays may lead some families to choose the DIY route, which can be far more economical while still allowing for meaningful personalization.

The level of personal involvement you desire also plays an important role. For some, creating the funeral program by hand offers a sense of connection and healing, providing a deeply personal way to honor a loved one. Finally, consider your expectations for quality. If a professionally polished and durable keepsake is the goal, a done-for-you service may offer the level of finish and presentation that best reflects the life being celebrated.

The Best of Both Worlds: Professional Design with Local Printing

For families who want a professionally crafted funeral program without the risk of shipping delays, a hybrid approach offers the ideal solution. This option involves working with an online service that handles the personalization and layout of your chosen template. The provider customizes the design with your selected photos, text, and formatting, then delivers a high-resolution, print-ready file straight to your inbox. This ensures your program has a polished, cohesive look created by experienced designers, while still allowing you to manage the timing and logistics of printing.

Once you receive the final file, you can take it to a local print shop or print it yourself using quality paper and equipment. This eliminates the uncertainty of courier schedules while giving you full control over when and how the materials are printed. While it may require a short trip to your printer, it provides peace of mind knowing your programs will be ready in time for the service. This "best of both worlds" approach is a smart, efficient choice for families who value both professional quality and reliable turnaround.

Making the Right Choice

Ultimately, the choice between done-for-you services and a DIY approach should align with what feels most appropriate and manageable for your family. Each path offers its own set of benefits, and neither is inherently better than the other—it's about what best suits your timeline, budget, creative confidence, and emotional needs during this time of remembrance.

A done-for-you service provides the assurance of professional quality and convenience, often alleviating stress during an already overwhelming period. Meanwhile, a DIY approach allows for deeply personal customization and can be a therapeutic, hands-on way to honor your loved one's life. Regardless of the method you choose, both options have the potential to produce a beautiful, meaningful funeral program that brings comfort to those who grieve and serves as a lasting tribute to a life well lived.

Chapter 8

Printing Options and Delivery

Once the design and content of a funeral program are complete, the next critical step is deciding how it will be printed and delivered. While the emotional and creative aspects of designing a tribute often take center stage, the logistics of printing play a significant role in ensuring that the program is available in time for the service, looks professional, and holds up as a cherished keepsake. Whether you're printing at home, using a local print shop, or ordering through an online provider, making the right printing choices will help bring your vision to life.

The first decision to consider is the printing method. Some families choose to print the program themselves, especially when time is limited or the service is informal. Home printing can be effective for short-run needs, but it's important to ensure your printer can handle high-quality graphics and fold neatly without smudging or misalignment. Using good paper stock is essential— 32 lb. paper is highly recommended for its ideal weight and structure. It provides a sturdy, professional feel without being too thick, and it helps prevent images or text from showing through the other side. Anything thinner may appear flimsy or allow ink bleed, which can diminish the appearance of the final piece.

Local print shops offer the advantage of in-person service and same-day turnaround in many cases. They are a practical choice for families who want to work with someone directly, and most allow you to bring your own specialty paper if you have a specific weight, texture, or color in mind. This flexibility can help you achieve the exact look and feel you want, particularly for more personalized or themed programs. Local printers also offer professional folding and finishing, which ensures crisp creases and proper alignment—something difficult to replicate consistently with a home printer.

For those who want to minimize stress and avoid running around town, many online printing services provide all-inclusive, done-for-you solutions. These services allow you to submit your content and images, and their in-house teams handle both the design and the printing. This can be especially helpful if you're short on time or aren't comfortable using design software yourself. Once approved, your order is printed and shipped directly to your door—or even to the funeral location. These services eliminate the need to coordinate multiple vendors and offer the convenience of managing everything from one place, often with fast turnaround options.

Online printing and delivery platforms are ideal for those who already have a completed program file and want reliable, high-quality results. These companies offer a variety of paper finishes, folding options, and quantities, and many allow for expedited shipping to meet tight timelines. Uploading a print-ready PDF file ensures your layout and fonts remain exactly as intended. As always, printing a test copy first—or reviewing a digital proof—is a wise step before placing a full order.

Not all online done-for-you services offer the same level of quality, and results can vary significantly depending on the provider. Some may use lower-grade materials or inconsistent printing methods, which can affect the overall presentation and durability of the memorial program. For such an important keepsake, it's essential to ensure that the final product meets your expectations in both appearance and craftsmanship.

Choosing a trusted, reputable source is the safest way to ensure a high-quality outcome. Look for services with positive customer reviews, clear examples of their work, and professional support throughout the process. A reliable provider will offer consistent print quality, timely delivery, and attentive customer care—giving you peace of mind during a time when details truly matter.

If you're distributing programs in person, consider printing extra copies to account for last-minute guests. Some families also choose to mail programs to those unable to attend or save them as part of a keepsake box. In this case, pairing the program with a note of thanks or memorial token can create an even more heartfelt gesture.

In addition to printed versions, a digital version of the program can be created to share online. This may be useful for live-streamed or virtual services, or for friends and family across long distances. A well-designed PDF can be emailed, hosted on a memorial page, or downloaded from a private link. Just ensure it's formatted for digital readability, using clear fonts and page layouts that adapt well to screens.

Whether printed at home, handled by a local provider, or produced by an all-in-one online service, the final delivery of the funeral program should reflect care and intention. The design, paper quality, and presentation all contribute to how the tribute is received and remembered. A thoughtfully printed funeral program serves as more than a handout—it becomes a physical extension of love and remembrance, something that family and friends will hold onto and treasure for years to come.

Chapter 9

After the Service – Preserving and Sharing the Tribute

The funeral or memorial program doesn't end its purpose when the service concludes. In fact, it often becomes more meaningful after the event. It transforms into a physical reminder of the ceremony, a cherished keepsake for loved ones, and a way to continue honoring the life it represents. This chapter focuses on what comes next—how to preserve, share, and repurpose the program so it continues to bring comfort and connection well beyond the day of remembrance.

Start by safeguarding the printed programs. If you've ordered extras, set aside several copies for safekeeping. Place one in a protective sleeve, memory chest, or archival box along with other mementos like the obituary, sympathy cards, and photographs. Laminating a program and placing it in a display frame can turn a practical document into a decorative memorial piece. This framed version can be placed on a shelf, mantle, or bedside table to quietly keep your loved one close.

Creating a digital version of the program ensures it lives on in formats that are easily shareable and accessible. Scan the program or export the design as a high-resolution PDF to store on a cloud drive, flash drive, or computer. Sharing this file with family members via email or private social media groups allows relatives who couldn't attend the service to still experience the tribute. You may also consider embedding a QR code onto thank-you cards, bookmarks, or memorial plaques that links to a downloadable copy of the program, ensuring a seamless connection to the content for years to come.

Some families choose to enhance the memory by turning the program into a digital slideshow or tribute video. Using the text, imagery, and structure from the printed layout, you can build a simple photo montage or animated video that narrates your loved one's story. This visual format can be shared on memorial websites, during anniversaries, or on social media as a way to honor and revisit the tribute in a dynamic way.

Incorporating the funeral program into an ongoing ritual of remembrance is another deeply meaningful option. Place a copy in a scrapbook alongside photos and stories from the day. Some families revisit the program on birthdays, death anniversaries, or holidays as part of a remembrance tradition. You can light a candle, recite a passage from the tribute, or simply reflect on the words shared. These gentle moments can become powerful, healing rituals that help keep the memory alive.

Extra printed copies can also serve as heartfelt gifts. Consider sending a program to close friends, caregivers, clergy, or distant relatives who had a meaningful connection to your loved one. Even a single copy mailed with a short note of thanks can deeply touch someone who shared in your grief or support. If you used a professional printing service, most providers allow you to reorder identical programs later, should you need more.

The funeral program you created is more than a document—

it's a legacy piece. With a few intentional steps, you can ensure it continues to reflect, honor, and preserve the unique life it celebrates. Whether framed, shared digitally, or lovingly stored, the program becomes a permanent tribute that connects generations, comforts hearts, and reminds others of a life beautifully lived.

Summary: Ways to Preserve and Share Your Tribute

- Store extra programs in a keepsake box, sleeve, or scrapbook
- Laminate and frame a copy for home display
- Scan or export to PDF for safe digital storage
- Share digital copies via email or private memorial sites
- Add QR codes to cards, plaques, or bookmarks
- Convert the program into a slideshow or tribute video
- Revisit the program during anniversaries or holidays
- Gift extra copies to extended family or close friends
- Reorder from professional print services if needed

Chapter 10

Frequently Asked Questions

Navigating the process of creating and distributing a funeral program can raise numerous questions, especially during a time of grief. This chapter aims to address some of the most commonly asked questions, providing clarity and guidance to help you make informed decisions.

1. What is the purpose of a funeral program?

A funeral program serves multiple purposes. It acts as a guide for attendees, outlining the order of service and providing information about the deceased. Additionally, it serves as a keepsake, preserving memories and honoring the life of the loved one. Including elements like photographs, personal stories, and meaningful quotes can make the program a cherished memento for family and friends.

2. How many copies of the funeral program should I print?

The number of copies needed depends on the expected number of attendees. It's advisable to print extra copies to accommodate unexpected guests and to have keepsakes for those unable to attend. Consider factors such as mailing programs to distant relatives or friends and providing copies to institutions or organizations the deceased was affiliated with.

3. Can I include personal touches in the funeral program?

Absolutely. Personalizing the program can make it more meaningful. You can include favorite poems, scriptures, quotes, or anecdotes that reflect the personality and life of the deceased. Incorporating hobbies, achievements, and cherished memories can provide comfort and a deeper connection for attendees.

4. What are the common sizes and formats for funeral programs?

Funeral programs typically come in various sizes and formats, including: **Bifold (single fold):** Creates four panels (front, inside left, inside right, back). **Trifold (two folds):** Offers six panels for more content. **Booklet:** Multiple pages stapled together, suitable for extensive content and numerous photos. The choice depends on the amount of information and personal preference.

5. Should I use color or black-and-white printing?

Color printing can enhance the visual appeal, especially when including photographs. However, black-and-white printing is a cost-effective alternative that can still be elegant and respectful. The decision should align with your budget and the desired aesthetic.

6. Is it necessary to include an obituary in the program?

Including an obituary is common but not mandatory. An obituary provides a narrative of the deceased's life, highlighting significant milestones, relationships, and accomplishments. If space is limited, a brief biography or timeline can also be effective.

7. Can I create and print the program myself?

Yes, many individuals choose to design and print funeral programs themselves. Utilizing templates and design software can facilitate the process. Ensure you have access to a quality printer and suitable paper stock, such as 32 lb. paper, to achieve a professional look.

8. Are there services that handle both design and printing?

Yes, several services offer comprehensive packages that include both design and printing. These services can alleviate stress by managing the entire process, ensuring a polished and timely result. This option is particularly beneficial when time or resources are limited.

9. How can I distribute the funeral program to those unable to attend?

For individuals who are unable to attend the service in person, there are thoughtful ways to ensure they still feel included and connected. One option is mailing physical copies of the funeral program to distant relatives and friends, providing them with a tangible keepsake they can hold onto. Digital distribution is another convenient method—sharing a PDF version of the program via email or uploading it to a memorial website allows recipients to view it instantly, no matter their location.

Social media can also be a valuable tool for broad outreach. Posting the program or a link to it on platforms like Facebook enables a wider network of family and friends to access and share in the remembrance, offering comfort and connection during a time when physical presence may not be possible.

10. What should I do with leftover programs?

Extra programs can be kept as keepsakes for family members, included in memory boxes, or archived for genealogical purposes. They can also be shared with organizations the deceased was involved with, such as churches, clubs, or workplaces.

Chapter 11

Final Thoughts and Resources

C reating a funeral program is more than just assembling pages of text and images; it's a heartfelt endeavor that encapsulates the essence of a loved one's life. Throughout this guide, we've explored various aspects of designing and producing a meaningful program, from choosing the right design to deciding between professional services and DIY approaches. As we conclude, let's reflect on the key takeaways and provide additional resources to assist you further.

Embracing the Journey

The process of crafting a funeral program is deeply personal. It offers an opportunity to celebrate the unique journey of the departed, sharing their stories, values, and the impact they've had on others. Whether you opt for a professionally designed program or take the DIY route, the most important element is the love and intention behind it.

Key Takeaways

- **Personalization Matters:** Tailoring the program to reflect the individual's personality and life story creates a more meaningful tribute.
- **Quality Over Quantity:** Focus on including content that truly honors the deceased, rather than overwhelming the program with excessive details.
- **Seek Support:** Don't hesitate to enlist the help of friends, family, or professionals to alleviate the burden during this emotional time.
- **Plan Ahead:** Whenever possible, preparing elements of the program in advance can reduce stress and ensure a smoother process.

Additional Resources

To further assist you in this journey, here are some of the best resources that offer templates, planning tools, and guidance:

The Funeral Program Site: A comprehensive platform offering both DIY funeral program templates and professional design and printing services. Their extensive collection includes various styles and themes to suit different preferences. funeralprogramsite.com

Canva Funeral Program Templates: Offers a variety of customizable templates to create personalized funeral programs. canva.com

My Wonderful Life: An online platform to plan and personalize your own funeral, easing the burden on loved ones. https://www.mywonderfullife.com

Angel & Dove Funeral Resources: Provides information, ideas, and planning tools to help create a funeral or celebration of life. https://www.angelanddove.com/pages/useful-funeral-resources

Dignity Memorial Planning Guide: Offers step-by-step guidance on planning a funeral, including choosing between burial and cremation. https://www.dignitymemorial.com

A Final Note

Remember, there is no one-size-fits-all approach to creating a

funeral program. Each life is unique, and the way we choose to celebrate it should be just as personal. Whether your design is simple or elaborate, handmade or professionally printed, what truly matters is that it speaks from the heart and reflects the spirit, values, and memories of your loved one.

This program is more than a schedule—it is a lasting tribute, a tangible piece of remembrance that offers comfort to those who grieve. It can be a source of healing, connection, and shared memory. Take the time you need to create something meaningful, lean on others for support if it becomes overwhelming, and most importantly, trust your instincts. There is no wrong way to honor a life that mattered.

Acknowledgments

This book would not have been possible without the countless families who have shared their stories, their strength, and their trust in me and The Funeral Program Site over the years. Your experiences inspired this guide, and your courage in the face of loss continues to shape everything we do.

I am deeply grateful to the dedicated team behind The Funeral Program Site—designers, writers, customer care specialists, and print professionals—who work with such compassion and excellence to serve families during life's most tender moments.

Thank you to my family and close friends for your unwavering support and encouragement as this book came to life. And to those navigating the journey of remembrance, I hope this guide brings you comfort, clarity, and confidence as you honor someone you love.

About the Author

 Christi Anderson is the founder of *The Funeral Program Site*, established in 1994 as a trusted resource for families and professionals seeking beautifully designed funeral programs and personalized memorial products. With a background in graphic design and a heart for serving others during life's most difficult moments, Christi has dedicated over two decades to helping people honor their loved ones with grace and meaning.

Since its founding, The Funeral Program Site has grown into a leading destination for high-quality funeral templates, printed memorials, and done-for-you design services. The site offers a wide range of styles—from classic to contemporary—suitable for every type of tribute, and provides support for both do-it-yourself projects and fully managed memorial solutions.

Through her work, Christi has guided thousands of families in creating thoughtful, elegant programs that tell a loved one's story with clarity and compassion. Her mission remains rooted in the belief that every life deserves to be remembered with dignity and personalization.

To explore available templates, custom design options, or to access helpful planning resources, visit: www.funeralprogramsite.com